COLDSTREAM BUILDING SNIPPETS

'CANS, QUOINS AND COURSERS'

COLDSTREAM BUILDING SNIPPETS

'CANS, QUOINS AND COURSERS'

Antony Chessell

Foreword by Andrew Douglas-Home

Published by Lulu

First published in 2010

Lulu Enterprises Ltd., 26-28 Hammersmith Grove
London W6 7BA www.lulu.com/uk

A catalogue record for this book is available from the British Library

ISBN 978-1-4457-8862-3

Typeset in Times New Roman

Printed and bound in Great Britain by Antony Rowe Ltd
Chippenham, Wiltshire

Front cover: gazebo (perhaps late eighteenth century), Henderson Park, Coldstream, overlooking the River Tweed. Cover design and photograph by the author

To the people of Coldstream and District, Scotland

CONTENTS

		Page
Illustrations		viii
Foreword		ix
Introduction		xi
1.	Sandstone and Styles	1
2	Walls and Wall Openings	21
3.	Roofs	33
4.	Doors and Windows	49
5.	Bits and Pieces	69
Glossary		94

ILLUSTRATIONS

The photographs are too many to list in a table of illustrations and they therefore appear:-

1. With unnumbered, explanatory captions, or
2. As 'thumbnails' with surrounding text

All photographs are from the author's collection

The author stresses that he has not trespassed on any private property in order to take photographs. Most of the building features are visible from roads, footpaths or other land with public access but in the few cases where it has been necessary to go on to private land, the owners have granted permission.*

*The Scottish Outdoor Access Code sets out rights and responsibilities for public access in terms of The Land Reform (Scotland) Act 2003, and lists the eight categories where there is no public right of access. One of these is houses and gardens, but if a house is located in a wider setting, Section 6 of the Act stipulates that there is no access on to land surrounding a house that is necessary to maintain privacy and undisturbed enjoyment of the house.

FOREWORD

By Andrew Douglas-Home

We are all guilty, I suspect, of rushing through life, most particularly in familiar surroundings, without ever quite taking the time to stop and look.

Coldstream's architectural history, its often old (some very old) and beautiful buildings, their quirks, their endless points of interest and detail, are all around us, yet how many of us truly appreciate them?

Antony Chessell's *Coldstream Building Snippets: 'Cans, Quoins and Coursers'* is learned and highly observant yet light-hearted and extremely easy to read. It describes all that is good about Coldstream's historic buildings and I trust that from now on whenever you and I walk along, for instance, the High Street, we will not only recognise but also appreciate the true significance of the buildings.

I have hugely enjoyed reading Antony's gentle ramble through Coldstream's built heritage and I commend it most highly. Readers will not only emerge the wiser, but, as Antony is most generously giving all the proceeds to the Community Centre, when you buy a copy you will be benefiting a community we, its residents, all love.

Andrew Douglas-Home
The Lees
Coldstream
June 2010

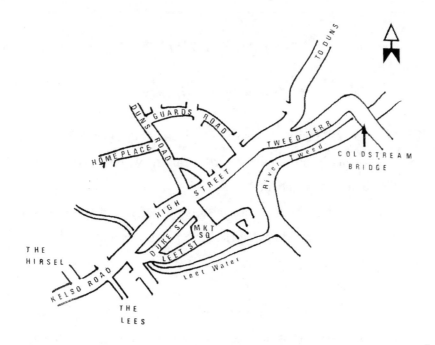

A simplified sketch map, showing the older part of Coldstream

This area includes most of the town's eighteenth and nineteenth century buildings; many of them are within the Conservation Area described on page xi, opposite. The distance covered by the map is roughly a mile from south-west to north-east. Not shown, but mentioned in the text, is Luke's Brae, which runs between High Street and Duke Street. Nursery Lane, also mentioned in the text, is the southmost 'curving' road between Duns Road and the High Street. Market Street is the street which connects the High Street with Market Square (old name, Market Place). Tweed Road is the road to the north-east of Market Square. Penitents Walk and Nun's Walk run close to the Leet Water and the River Tweed respectively.

INTRODUCTION

O n the title page, a 'can' is a Scottish term for a chimney pot made of fired clay or metal, on top of a chimney stack and connected to a flue. A 'quoin' is the exterior angle of a wall or a cornerstone set in a brick or a stone wall that provides structural stability and often a decorative appearance. A 'courser' is a regular squared stone, dressed (meaning prepared or finished) or roughly dressed, laid with others in courses (horizontal layers) to build a wall.

Coldstream has a surprisingly rich heritage of vernacular Scottish buildings for such a small town or large village, and this book sets out to describe many of the distinctive external features and techniques that have gone into their construction. The old buildings that demonstrate these traditional construction features are mostly located within Coldstream's Conservation Area covering Duns Road (part), High Street, Duke Street, Leet Street, Market Street, Market Square (Place), Tweed Road and the narrow pends and closes which lead off them. There are also farmhouses, cottages and outbuildings in the countryside around Coldstream that are no less detailed in their construction and decoration than many of the urban buildings. Some of the buildings have fallen on hard times over the years from weathering, and damaged stonework, in particular, is in constant need of repair.

COLDSTREAM BUILDING SNIPPETS

The author has always had a professional interest in buildings but this is not an architectural or surveying handbook and neither is it a history of the buildings or town of Coldstream. The history of the town is already covered in *Second to None: A History of Coldstream*, published by Coldstream and District Local History Society, 2010. My book is intended as a 'potterer's' guide to building features in Coldstream, in keeping with my family tradition. Present and previous generations of the family have sketched, painted, and jotted things down in notebooks when 'pottering' around streets, buildings and churchyards throughout Britain, often with their heads in the air and sometimes a danger to themselves and to others. It is amazing what can be discovered; we tend to take in buildings at a glance when we are passing, but it is worth stopping and taking time to examine the extent of the detailing that has gone in to their construction and decoration.

Coldstream is unarguably a Scottish town, despite being so close to England. This is reflected in the character of its people who are Scottish Borderers and quite distinct in accent and dialect from their near neighbours in Northumberland. The buildings too, are demonstratively Scottish and pertain to styles found in Berwickshire, Roxburghshire and the Lothians that would be out of place in a Northumbrian setting. This strong demarcation occurs immediately after crossing the River Tweed over Coldstream Bridge from Cornhill-on-Tweed in Northumberland (the English/Scottish Border runs along the median line of the river) and arises for geographical and historical reasons.

INTRODUCTION

I have to be careful here because the northern Northumbrians are Borderers too and from the same stock as their neighbours living in the Scottish Borders. The Battle of Carham in 1018 had established Scotland's hold over the Lothians and Borders, but the Border Line was first fixed in 1237, by the Treaty of York. The line was the subject of much cross-border conflict and, from 1249 onwards, any disregard of the Border Line was subject to inquests held under the Border Laws, the *Leges Marchiarum*, enforced by English and Scottish March Wardens. Because of grievances and suspicions, history has dictated that, politically, the Scottish and the English Borderers have turned their backs on each other and that distinctions were maintained even after the Union of the Crowns in 1603. That is why, even now, people living a mile apart on either side of the river speak either a Scottish Border dialect or a Northumbrian dialect.

For hundreds of years, Coldstream occupied a strategic position where the English and Scottish armies forded the river on their expeditions north or south. Today, Coldstream's strong feeling of identity is emphasised every August during Civic Week with the Flodden Rideout, commemoration of the Scottish dead on the field of battle in 1513 and commemoration of the burial of the Scottish nobility on or near Tweed Green, below Coldstream Priory.

My thanks are due to the people of Coldstream and District who have allowed me to wander around their buildings, taking photographs and notes. Special thanks go to my wife, Gwen, for her interest, help and encouragement during preparation of the book.

Antony Chessell, Coldstream, Scottish Borders, 2010

Detail of Coldstream Bridge, 1763-1766, architect John Smeaton, showing coursed sandstone facing stones and inset roundel of basalt rubble surrounded by moulded voussoirs and keystones

1

Sandstone and Styles

Much of the stone for the traditional buildings in Coldstream and round about, came out of the two disused quarries on the east side of Duns Road opposite the junction with Home Place, but some came from other quarries in the area, including two at Swinton. These local quarries produced sandstone, which is known as 'freestone' because it can be easily cut without splitting. Sandstone in Berwickshire and Roxburghshire varies in colour according to the constituent minerals within it and this will depend upon where it is located and also on its geological period. Colour can range from deep red as seen, for example, at Ayton Castle and around the doorway at Smailholm Tower, through to a light 'biscuit' colour at Coldstream and Swinton, where the sandstone was formed in the late Carboniferous era, over 300 million years ago. There are many other shades including the subtle pink sandstone from Swinton, used in the Scottish National War Memorial at Edinburgh Castle. Other building stones were used in the Borders, such as the greywacke sandstone known as 'whinstone', a term which is also commonly applied to the hard, black, basalt lavas of volcanic origin from the early Carboniferous period (the Silurian era, over 415 million years ago) found in the Kelso area and seen in some of the houses in Birgham, in

Light, 'biscuit' colour, sandstone walling off Duns Road, typical of the building stone used in Coldstream's 18th and 19th century buildings

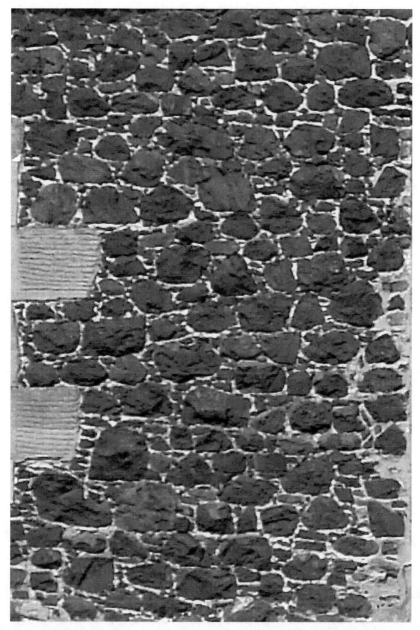

Black, basalt walling of volcanic origin, Main Street, Birgham

the main walls at Smailholm and in many houses in Gordon. There are very few examples of basalt in Coldstream but it is possible to find stones incorporated into sandstone house and boundary walls, for example in Nursery Lane and within the roundels on Coldstream Bridge. Basalt can give a sombre appearance to a street and is more difficult to work, but it is hardwearing and not subject to surface fragmentation or 'spalling' as has happened with many of the sandstone buildings in Coldstream.

A walk around old Coldstream will soon reveal the wide variety of buildings from the eighteenth and nineteenth centuries. Most of the houses have two or more storeys, but there are some single storey cottages reminiscent of the earliest houses, such as in Luke's Brae off the High Street (see below). The first buildings in the

town must have grown up next to the important ford over the River Tweed near the mouth of the Leet Water and would have had a wattle and daub framework with thatched roofs of straw, reed, heather or turf. They were joined in the twelfth century by the stone-built priory and the buildings that grew up around it, but the earliest settlement of Coldstream as we know it, was probably built in the seventeenth century around and close to the market square; as a result of this development, the parish church at Lennel was transferred to a site in the new Coldstream.

After the turnpike road was built in the 1760s, from the new Coldstream Bridge over the Leet Water Bridge and north to Edinburgh, land was feued along the High Street and the village started to develop to the north and east. The early houses would still have been thatched and, by the beginning of the nineteenth century many must have been considered as inadequate, because a substantial number of the old houses and other buildings in what was becoming a much larger village, were pulled down and rebuilt, whilst others were altered and re-roofed with slates or tiles. Many buildings from the eighteenth century can still be seen, whereas others from that century and earlier are hidden as central or 'core' parts of enlarged and altered properties.

The early eighteenth century single storey houses were very low, simple in layout and external appearance and the door and windows were not necessarily symmetrical. It is not possible to be precise about the development of house styles in the Borders as this depended very much upon area and individual circumstances. However, during the eighteenth century and into the nineteenth century, the single storey became higher and windows became symmetrical on either side of a central front door.

At the beginning of the nineteenth century, thatch was replaced by slates or tiles and the floor level raised inside to prevent rainwater running across the floor from the street. Ceiling heights and roof levels had to be raised even more to compensate and one or more front steps had to be constructed from the street up to the new ground floor level. Stone chimneys were added and gable ends were often raised above the roof slope, instead of the roof overlapping the gables.

Single storey cottage, perhaps late 18th century, with symmetrical door and windows and raised front step, Lennel

Three, single storey cottages (perhaps early 19th century) with chimneys, since converted to one cottage, Kelso Road. The left hand window was originally a door.

6

The next stage of cottage development was for the roof height to be raised even more to accommodate an attic room, perhaps with a roof light in the slope of the roof, but often this was followed by a need to improve the attic space and to increase the light by adding dormer windows. The dormers could be entirely within the roof space, which meant that the attic had no vertical walls other than the sides of the dormer windows. However, by raising the eaves height yet again, the resultant half storey could be partly within the main walls and partly within the sloping roof space, therefore reducing the amount of 'lie-in' of the ceilings. Initially, access to the attic would have been by a ladder through a ceiling opening or hatch but later improvements would have demanded a proper staircase, often having a steep angle because of constricted access to a sloping attic space.

A house with a ground floor and a habitable room within the sloping roof, as opposed to an attic storeroom, is called a 1½ storey house and the house in the High Street (see below, left) falls into this category, as evidenced by the three dormer windows set partly into

the attic space. From 1750 onwards, houses were built with two storeys or more and, again, there are many examples within Coldstream's conservation area of simple yet good cottages and houses that fall into this category, usually built as terraced properties.

The two-storey end of terrace cottage in Duke Street (see below) may be of eighteenth century construction. Note the

asymmetrical door and windows. The style of windows may have changed if the cottage was built in the 1700s, but the windows are still good examples of traditional Victorian 4-pane windows (see Chapter 4: Doors and Windows). The wide variety of eighteenth and early nineteenth century building styles is visible in the oldest part of the town, with good examples to be seen in Duke Street and Leet Street; naturally, all the houses have been modified over time.

1 storey cottage with modernised attic, adjoining 2 storey cottages, and other properties, Duke Street, c. 1800 onwards.

A terrace of early 19th century two storey cottages in Duns Road

Early 19th century houses in the High Street, having more formal door surround features (see Chaps. 2 & 4 for openings and doors)

Houses became more stylish as the nineteenth century progressed through the Georgian and Victorian eras, giving much more commodious living space, higher ceilings and grander, classical and formal external features, with more elaborate doors and windows and other decorative embellishments. In Coldstream and other Border towns, houses of 2½ storeys and 3 storeys or more, or shops with houses above, were built during the nineteenth century, the increase in height often being determined by the smaller feus in the main streets.

19th century 3 storey terraced houses in Market Square (Place).

Unlike the Market Square houses above, most larger houses would have had even more steps up to an impressive front door, to minimise the trampling in of mud or to prevent flooding. Georgian features, such as larger full height windows, were incorporated into many of the houses in Coldstream High Street, which were also built with basement staff accommodation that necessitated flyover stairs across the well and steps down from the street, requiring protective iron balustrades and railings (see below). Some of these basements were extended beneath the street to provide space for storage or coal.

Early 19th century 2½ storey and basement houses (here the dormers are entirely within the attic space) with flyover steps and more recently painted frontages; some of the dormer windows have been modified

The later Victorian period produced large houses with high ceiling heights and projecting bay windows with ornamentation such as roof or dormer finials and carved wood or stone roof brackets. Because the older houses had already claimed the central area, the Victorian 'villas' tended to be sited around or peripheral to the centre. These were detached, semi-detached or terraced houses and good examples of all three types can be seen in Coldstream, including those at the eastern end of the High Street and in Tweed Terrace.

Late 19th century, terraced villas, Tweed Terrace

The nineteenth and early twentieth centuries saw the building or rebuilding of public buildings in a wide variety of styles, many of which reflected previous architectural eras, if not always in a

conventional way. For example, the former Coldstream West United Church, now the Community Centre, was built in 1907 in the Perpendicular style (say from 1380-1550) with shallow arched windows and unfussy tracery, set in random rubble walling with dressed

stonework (see above). It has a dominant and strong looking tower; the crenellated parapets, lower tower windows and other features are more in keeping with the Arts and Crafts movement of late Victorian and Edwardian times (see the 'Arts and Crafts' blind window, above).

The Parish Church in the High Street, rebuilt in 1906-8,

retains the late eighteenth century tower and is difficult to categorise in terms of architectural style although it has a Presbyterian and Scottish feel to it (see left). The former Coldstream Free

Church in Victoria Street (now the Eildon Centre) was built in 1846, but was changed considerably by its 1891 enlargement; it is noticeable for the prominent clock tower (see previous page, bottom, right) with its distinctive four-gabled roof and gothic windows. St. Mary and All Souls Episcopal Church situated in Lennel Road (see below), was only built in 1913-14, but its simple apse and rectangular form harks back to the Early English Gothic period with its unadorned pointed arches and buttressed walls.

Having said that this is not an architectural handbook, I have

now broken my own rule by mentioning the Early English Gothic period (say from 1180-1280) and the Perpendicular Gothic period (say from 1380-1550), not to mention the Arts and Crafts era (say from 1880-1910). My justification is that I wanted to show that later public buildings often imitate earlier styles and it is

not surprising to see that Coldstream's churches dating from the eighteenth to the twentieth centuries incorporate features copied from medieval church architecture.

Non-secular public buildings often incorporate classical features in imitation of Greek and Roman architecture in order to give them status. The former Mechanics' Institute (see above), now the Library and Registrar's office, was built in 1861-3 with a frontage which echoes a classical temple. Four pilasters (square columns which are set into the wall) enclose three bays of the building with a frieze above, supporting a triangular pediment. Unlike many Greek or Roman temples, however, the design is very simple and there are no carved decorations on the frieze or on the tympanum, which is the area within the triangular pediment. The capitals at the top of the columns are also understated.

The Halifax Bank of Scotland building, originally the British Linen Company Bank (see right), built in 1891, has a classical doorway with two partly fluted freestanding columns on plinths, supporting Ionic capitals and a rectangular frieze and balustrade.

Not all public buildings or former public buildings in Coldstream looked

back in time. For example, the Police Station, built in 1868 in Victorian villa style (see left), the former Cottage Hospital now the Dental Surgery in Kelso Road, built in 1888 (see next page, left) and the former North Public School and Schoolhouse in Home Place (see next page, right), built between 1858 and 1900, are all unashamedly Victorian and do not borrow from previous eras, although recent alterations have caused the Victorian integrity to be lost on the dental surgery frontage.

An important publicly owned landmark that does borrow some features from the past despite also being up to date at the time of its construction, is Coldstream Bridge. The bridge was designed by

John Smeaton and built between 1773 and 1776 and is a fine example of advanced 18th century engineering, but Smeaton inset eight distinctive roundels in the pier spandrels, which are reminiscent of the Italian Renaissance (of classical principles, say the end of the thirteenth century to the end of the sixteenth century) and the oculus windows of the English Baroque period (say the late seventeenth and early eighteenth centuries). He also used classical dentils (i.e. like teeth) below the parapet. However, the Charles Marjoribanks Monument in Tweed Terrace, 1834 (with replacement statue of 1874), is in pure classical Greek or Roman style with its fluted Doric column; standing proudly on top of his plinth of laurel wreaths, 'Charlie' might well be a Roman emperor (see left).

Classical and other period features also appear in grander domestic architecture in Scotland, but there are not many examples in Coldstream. The Hirsel, although impressive, is not a building exhibiting grandiose architectural design. It is a large, historic, but unpretentious eighteenth century house with nineteenth century additions, set in magnificent surroundings.

The Lees, showing the rotunda with Ionic capitals and dentilation to the cornice above the frieze (see next page)

17

By contrast, The Lees was built in 1770 in classical style but was mostly demolished in 1980 leaving only the central bow of the east frontage and a reused portico. The bow has recently been extended to form a rotunda with conical roof to which additions have been made in sympathetic style. The eastern, original side of the circular core of the house has classical round and square pilasters with Ionic capitals supporting a frieze and a cornice with a row of dentils. The classical theme is repeated in Lees Lodge on the Kelso Road (see below) that reflects the architecture of the main house, although on a much smaller scale. Here, the front door is flanked by partly inset plain columns surmounted by Ionic capitals. The lodge also has a dentilated cornice below the roof and gutters.

Lees Lodge: entrance columns with Ionic capitals; corbel dentils

The Lees estate is also home to the octagonal temple on the bank of the River Tweed (see next page). Like the original house, it dates from the late eighteenth century. The columns are set on panelled plinths but have a simple outline with plain Doric capitals.

There are steps up to the raised floor and there is an attractive bell roof with a ball finial.

The very different buildings mentioned in this chapter give a glimpse of the progression and regression in styles from the eighteenth century onwards, but the more specific building details described in the following chapters should help to define the essential character of Coldstream's buildings. This is Scottish, but with a regional flavour determined by Coldstream's location within Berwickshire and the Borders. Some people suggest that there is a grimness to Scottish towns and villages. This can be true and is more likely where the local stone is of a darker colour and where there are no trees, which are not traditional in Scottish streets or squares. Coldstream is fortunate in the lighter colour of its stone, its location next to the River Tweed and Tweed Green and because surrounding greenery penetrates to the centre of the town by way of gardens and playing fields. Some recently planted trees and raised flowerbeds in Market Square have also helped a little to soften the hard landscaping and the car parking in that area.

The townscape within Coldstream's conservation area has changed during the last one hundred years, although not as much as might be expected. Leaving aside changes to road surfacing, street lamps, street signs and modern shop fronts (although Coldstream has few of these and has retained many old frontages), it is interesting to compare present street scenes with those shown in old photographs. The most obvious difference is that many buildings have had their stonework painted or harled, whereas old views, for example of the High Street, show a continuous facade of uncovered stonework. Harling is a Scottish term for an exterior coating that is applied to weatherproof the stonework. In England, it is called rendering. It is a plastered base coat of lime on to which thrown pebbles can be added for protection and appearance. It may then be limewashed in a chosen colour. Buildings in Coldstream may have been painted or harled for cosmetic reasons but, over the years, many buildings have suffered from damaged stonework and harling has been applied as a cheaper alternative to cutting out and replacing stonework.

2

Walls and Wall Openings

In this chapter I want to look at the stonework used for building construction in Coldstream and district. In the quarry or in the workshops, the stonemasons cut and worked the stone into two kinds of building block, firstly, dressed sandstone in regular, rectangular blocks and, secondly, roughly squared sandstone blocks used for less formal walling. In addition, builders used stones gathered from the fields, which were uncut or perhaps lightly trimmed, for use in random rubble walling. An important rule is that, because sandstone is a sedimentary stone i.e. laid down millions of years ago in a series of deposited bedding layers at the bottom of a sea, lake or river, the building stones should always be built into a wall with the bedding layers or planes at right angles to the face of the wall to resist weathering. This usually  means as horizontal bedding planes, but they can be vertical for some features. These bedding planes can be seen in the photograph of a worn section of wall (see above). If they were parallel to the wall face, they could easily split away like the layers of an onion.

The finest dressed sandstone was either polished to create a smooth surface known as ashlar, or tooled to give an attractive decorated surface. Dressed stonework had narrow mortar joints (see below), with ashlar having the very finest mortar joints. Trafalgar

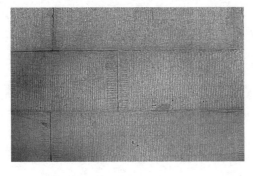

House, built in 1830-32, is a good example of how large, squared and polished ashlar blocks, built in regular courses and with very fine mortar joints, create a grand style for a particular purpose. The Manse, as it then was, reflected the importance in Coldstream of the parish and its minister. Other public and commercial buildings, some of which have already been mentioned in relation to their style, also had finely worked ashlar masonry to show off their importance, such as the Mechanics Institute (now the Library and Registrar's office), the British Linen Company Bank (now Halifax Bank of Scotland), and the Commercial Bank (now a private house) all in the High Street, and the Bank of Scotland (now Victoria Lodge) in Victoria Street. There are also many examples of domestic buildings that were built with ashlar frontages to demonstrate their high quality and the status of their owners and/or occupiers. The quality could also extend to buildings that were important, but ancillary to, the main house, such as the lodge to The Lees, on Kelso Road, which has been mentioned before.

By contrast, many of the oldest houses and cottages in the town were built quite simply, for purely domestic and ancillary uses.

They may have random rubble masonry of varying sizes, not built in regular courses, but functional and unpretentious—just right for the job, and attractive in their own right.

2 storey and attic (with dormers) houses with ashlar walling, High Street

2 storey and attic house with random rubble walling, High Street

23

Random rubble boundary walling set in lime mortar

Other houses in the town show the many gradations between random rubble and ashlar, in both coursed and uncoursed masonry. All the stonework in Coldstream was originally laid and pointed in lime mortar, easily recognised by its soft and gritty appearance (see above). In recent years, repairs and re-pointing have often been carried out using cement mortar, which is cheaper and offers a harder and smoother finish. Unfortunately, as well as not looking quite right on old buildings, the use of cement mortar can be a false economy as its strength does not accommodate small movements of the building, without cracking. Also, its impermeability prevents the escape of moisture which has soaked into the stonework and cannot then find its way out through the joints; this can lead to internal dampness and stone decay including the very visible surface 'spalling.' The use of more expensive 'breathable' lime mortar will often be the cheapest option in the long run. In my view it will always give a more attractive finish.

Random rubble walling with hard cement mortar pointing

Polished ashlar stones are always laid in very regular courses with fine joints, as already mentioned. Dressed or undressed stones may be given a variety of tooled finishes on their faces, the simplest and probably the most common being 'droving' or 'broaching' which consists of a series of fairly narrow, horizontal, almost parallel cut lines, produced by a hammer and a toothed chisel or mason's 'boaster'.

Rubble stonework in lime mortar with roughly done 'stugging' (top stones) and 'droving' or 'broaching' (bottom stone)

Another common finish is 'stugging' (see above) where the face of the stone is covered by depressions made by a mason's punch. Other dressed stones may not be bedded to the same accuracy as ashlar (see above) and their faces may be left with a less perfect finish. They may

26

be laid more or less in horizontal courses with small squared stones called 'snecks' (see photo on previous page) being inserted in order to infill any gaps or make up the levels.

Random rubble walling may also be laid in roughly levelled

courses (known as random rubble built to courses, see left) of more than the height of one stone, again using snecks or rough 'pinnings' to make up the course levels (see left). In the example shown here, the wall includes some re-used and rather worn stones that have been droved and stugged. Alternatively, random rubble walling may not be laid in courses at all. In this form of construction, structural stability is obtained by skilful laying of the stones in the same way as for drystone (or drystane)

walls, assisted by adhesion of the lime mortar between them. Sometimes, the rubble stones may be laid in such a way, or even split, so that their flat surfaces appear on

the face of the wall. That may be the case in this boundary wall at Home Park (see above, right) where large field gatherings or reused stones seem to have been used showing their flat surfaces.

Random rubble walling in buildings is usually enhanced by

incorporating ashlar or other dressed stones known as 'quoins' at corners of the building and 'rybats' around window and door openings. As well as providing decorative enhancement, there is also an important practical reason for this because it is necessary to provide strong and sharp corners to a building and to give even surrounds to door and window openings for easier joinery installation. The long and short faces of the quoins or rybats usually alternate, in which case the long face is called the 'outband' and the short face, the 'inband'.

Dressed stones commonly have smooth or tooled margin strips at their edges that provide a decorative feature but which, again, also have a practical purpose. For example, making a margin on the outer edge of the block would help to prevent any damage to the sharp corner or 'arris' that might otherwise be caused by stugging or other surface tooling of the stone. In the example (see above), the random rubble wall has dressed stone quoins that, starting from the top, are outband, inband, outband, inband. The quoins have been stugged and have droved margins visible to the right of the rhone pipe. In this case, there has been some recent use of cement mortar.

The photograph (see next page), of a wall feature in Market

Street shows the mason's skill in creating a bevel at the corner of a wall where a sharp arris might have caused a nuisance or danger to pedestrians turning the corner in that particular location. All the curved and flat stones have droved margins and this gives a particularly pleasing decorative effect on the concave and convex surfaces (even without the fairy lights!).

A modified version of ashlar walling can be seen on two buildings in the High Street where the blocks of stone are separated by wide, recessed joints in a form of

masonry known as rustication. The first example (see left) shows the front wall of a basement with a window opening.

The rustification effect adds decorative emphasis to the elevation and, in this case, the lintel has been carved to imitate the wedge-shaped 'voussoirs' usually found above an arched opening. The other example (see above right) is at ground floor shop window level; the stonework has been painted over.

In the same way as the end or angle of a wall needed to be finished and strengthened by the use of quoins, so did window and door openings need 'rybats', partly to strengthen the opening but also to enable timber frames to be installed without gaps. Again, this was particularly important if the main construction of the wall was in random rubble. The window at The Hirsel outbuildings (see below)

has dressed outbands and inbands for the rybats with random rubble built to courses on either side and a stone lintel and stone sill above and below the window. The upright rybats can also be known as 'starts' and the horizontal rybats as 'tails'; the photograph shows a lightly droved margin around the window, droved lintel and sill and droved starts and tails. The window frame is 'rebated' (partly hidden) behind the face of the wall and the visible return face of the stonework is known as the 'reveal'. This window is chosen as an example of the simplest treatment that can be applied to window or door openings, but even here, the mason has used a decorative finish with droved margins to rybats, lintel and sill and more heavily droved starts and tails.

There are many examples in the town of more elaborate treatments of door and window openings where the mason has been commissioned to add chamferings, mouldings and other carved features. The doorway of this nineteenth century house at the east end of the High Street (see left) has a great deal of carved stonework projecting from the wall face and even the window opening has raised rybats, lintel and sill, standing out from the wall.

Brickwork was not often used as a main construction material in Coldstream. This was because there was a plentiful supply of local stone, and the clays used in the many Lothian brickworks were often not of sufficiently high quality to be used for the face of a building. However, during the nineteenth century, there were many red brick outhouses built in the town and examples can be seen down the back closes. Some chimneystacks were built of red bricks, but the Lothian brickworks also produced light yellow 'common' bricks and these were used more often for chimneystacks in Coldstream because they toned in with the colour of the stone. The reason for their use will be covered in the next chapter.

3

Roofs

When walking around the town, it is worth looking up at the varied roofs and roof lines of the old buildings, taking care not to be crossing the road at the same time! This difference in height and type of roof along a street frontage is one of the reasons why old buildings can have such an appeal, compared with modern and more uniform buildings. The roof lines in the photograph below and the variety of building styles, all add to the interest of the High Street.

Different roof heights & buildings, High Street, east of 'Toun Heid'

COLDSTREAM BUILDING SNIPPETS

In Coldstream, the chimneystacks above roof level are often  entirely built in brickwork or are topped by several courses of brickwork below the chimney pots or 'cans'. The workshop or former bothy in Duns Road (see left) shows this form of construction being used on a simple building, but the technique was used on all kinds of buildings in the town. The mixture of stone and yellowish 'common' brick for chimneystacks is therefore very characteristic of Coldstream and the eastern Borders but, as has been mentioned, red brick was sometimes used instead. It may seem strange that the stonework was not carried up to the full chimney height. However, compared with relatively soft sandstone, brick is better able to withstand the temperature of fumes because it is a fired material and can cope with the intense heating and cooling cycles and the chemical reactions of hot flue gases. Bricks are also easier for building around complex flues. This chimneystack (see right) rises above the roof slopes in stone,  with the upper part built in brickwork; the projecting brick 'oversailing' course relieves the rectangular shape of the stack.

It has been mentioned that the straw, reed, heather or turf

thatch roofs were superseded or replaced after about 1800 by non-combustible slates or by clay pantiles. Thick and chunky natural Scottish slates (see left) would have been the first choice in Coldstream—these might have come from elsewhere in the Borders such as the Peebles area, but later would have come from the West Highlands, such as the deep blue-black slates from Ballachulish in Lochaber, or perhaps the midnight blue slates from the Hill of Foudland in Aberdeenshire. Thinner purple slates from Wales and green or grey slates from Westmoreland (which were easier to split than Scottish slates) were also used, particularly later on, for repairs. On some old outbuildings in the town, you can see a multi-coloured, patched result.

The traditional method in Scotland was to 'head nail' with one nail through the top of the slate on to flat boarding or 'sarking' with the horizontal boards butted together, as opposed to the English method of slating with two nails on to lath strips. The boarding provided more insulation, but still allowed some ventilation between the sarking boards. The single nail method meant that the slates were susceptible to being lifted by the wind, but the heavier weight of

35

Scottish slates counteracted this, with the added advantage that each slate could be swung aside easily for replacement of other damaged slates. The Scottish climate usually dictates a slope of at least 40°.

It was also good practice in Scotland to use a system of graduated or diminished course slating with the largest and heaviest slates at the bottom of the roof where they were best placed to withstand weathering and greater flow of rainwater and where their weight would be taken more by the wall. As the slater moved up the slope, the slates would decrease in size, row by row with the smallest slates at the top. As well as having a practical function, the graduated

style has a pleasing effect, but it does not seem to have been used very much, if at all, in Coldstream. The ridge would be capped by a lead or zinc flashing but clay ridge tiles were also used which, in Victorian times, often had moulded scallops or similar decorative treatment with dormer and porch roofs having clay, timber or iron finials, as with this example (see above) at the former Police Station at Court House Place.

The other form of roofing was the use of handmade red clay pantiles with triangular, or third, or half round, clay ridge tiles. Pantiles were cheaper than slates because they could be sourced locally and they were often used for cottages and subsidiary buildings, but there was no hard and fast rule. Pantiles are not plentiful in Coldstream, being more common in towns and villages in the

Lothians and Fife. However, although slate predominates, pantiles were used in Coldstream and Lennel on the roofs of houses, cottages and other buildings, like the hidden seventeenth century former Home Farm building behind Howden's shop, or in the town's closes and pends. They are also found on rural buildings in the surrounding area.

Handmade pantiles on the roof of a store at Lennel

The colour of pantiles varied from orange, through red to black, depending upon the origin of the clay. Over time, the tiles weathered and developed a patina, as well as attracting lichens. Unlike slates, pantiles were not nailed down on to sarking boards; instead, nibs on their top edges were hooked over wooden battens that were nailed on to the rafters. The tiles overlapped the row below and also overlapped laterally, but the single lapping and curly 'S' shape meant that roof spaces could be very draughty compared with slate roofs. This was despite the liberal use of lime mortar underneath the tiles in between the battens and rafters (known as 'parging') and also as thick bedding layers in the lower courses of tiles. Clay ridge tiles too, were bedded in lime mortar and, to improve draught proofing even further, it was common practice to lay two or three rows of slates nearest to the eaves, with the rest of the roof slope being laid in

Pantiled roofs between Tweed Road and Gowanlea, showing the two lowest courses laid in slate to improve draught-proofing

pantiles. Modern machine-made pantiles are much more regular and

do not have the variation in shape and colour of handmade tiles but eventually even these will weather, although they will never have the same character. In the example above, the roof slope extends over the gable ends, but often the gables of a building would be built up above roof height (see above) to form a sloping 'skew' topped by coping-stones.

Skews vary in style but, in Coldstream, they tend to be fairly plain; the one above has a decorative roll at the apex. The lowest stone of the skew is known as the skewputt and, again in Coldstream, these are usually plain. However, there are examples of simple scroll skewputts in the High Street and at Tweed Green (see below left). The crow or 'corbie stepped' gable skew was not common in Coldstream, but this one (see below right) can be seen from Guards Road.

Where slates or tiles abutted a raised gable end or the wall of another building, the joint would be sealed by a lead or zinc 'flashing' or, particularly for pantiled roofs, by using a mortar 'fillet'. Instead of terracotta tiles on a ridge or on a 'piended' roof (i.e. at the sloping joints between the end 'hip' and the front and back

roof slopes coming down from the ridge), a lead or zinc capping could be used (see above, on the sloping piends).

From the beginning of the nineteenth century, the mass production of cast iron rhones (gutters in England) and rhone pipes meant that these could be easily fitted to all buildings. Even so, pantiled roofs on outbuildings or poorer or older buildings often still discharged rainwater directly on to the ground. Cast iron goods could be sourced in Scotland, which helped to keep the cost down for general use. Cast iron is very tough in compression, but is brittle in tension and cannot withstand heavy knocks but, subject to this, it is very hard-wearing; it does, however, require regular painting to prevent rusting. The casting process allowed for quite elaborate mouldings and decorations on rhones and brackets and on the hopper heads at the top of the rhone pipes, but standard rhones just had a half-round profile with circular section rhone pipes. Coldstream has examples of the simplest profiles, but also has examples of more elaborate cast moulded profiles used on many buildings.

In the case of a 1½ or 2½ storey house with dormers only

partly in the roof space, it meant that because the eaves line was half way up the dormer windows, the cast iron rhones had to pass across the front of the windows. This rather unusual feature is found more often in other parts of Scotland, but there is an example in Leet Street (see above) and two other ones in the High Street. The house shown, also has a moulded hopper at the top of the rhone pipe, taking water from the half-round section rhone.

Chimneystacks on seventeenth and eighteenth century cottages often did not have cans and finished at the mortar or cement 'flaunching' (capping). However, it was soon realized that cans were necessary to improve the updraught and that one chimney stack could support a number of cans, each connected to its own flue from a particular fireplace below and set in the flaunching (see right).

Handmade clay-fired cans were manufactured throughout Scotland and became decorative as well as functional. There are many styles

visible in Coldstream from the simple cylindrical type, to rectangular and octagonal cans, through to much more elaborate moulded designs such as the tall fluted cans seen at High Street/ Guards Road (see above). An unusual duo can be seen in the archaeological museum at The Hirsel (see left). It is not surprising that such antique, decorative cans are often purchased from reclamation yards for use as garden ornaments and planters.

Coldstream roofs also have a variety of ventilators and cowls

which, as well as having a useful purpose, also provide a decorative feature that is in keeping with the architecture of the building. The Victorian metal ventilator (see left) is one of a number on the roof of the old school (now workshops) seen from Home Park. Judging by the twigs, the chicken wire placed across the ventilator has not deterred some determined birds from attempting to build a nest. A more utilitarian vent can be seen on the roof of outbuildings at The Hirsel (see right). The need to improve the updraught on chimney flues can lead

to some very strange shapes and the example shown here (see left) is no exception. Whereas the right hand can is shaped like a champagne glass (sort of!) on a stalk, the left hand can has sloping side vents as well as an 'H' design cowl, to create the maximum draught.

In other parts of the Borders and in the Lothians, there is an emphasis on elaborately decorated and carved timber 'verges' or bargeboards on the gable ends of buildings or on porch roofs. Verges occur at the top of a gable wall where, because the roof covering extends over

the wallhead, there is no stone skew. Decorative woodwork can also be found above dormer windows or on porch roofs. Coldstream does not have much carved woodwork but there are a few examples of restrained decoration such as the example (see above) of a Victorian roof on the corner of Guards Road. This is a simple but attractive zig zag pattern on the verge, above a hipped roof to a bay window.

At the former Police Station at the top of Court House Place,

there is a much later porch added to the front of the original eighteenth century building (see left). The porch has a carved timber verge with a decorative truss and collar beam. Towards the eastern end of the High Street, it is worth glancing upwards to see two late Victorian dormer windows with carved verges and brackets to the projecting roof slopes (see next page). They also incorporate decorative trusses.

Dormer windows, High Street. Note also the brick upper courses to the chimneystack with dentilated brick corbelling

Two cottages at the Leet Water Bridge, High Street

I have mentioned roofs with front and back slopes bounded by gable ends, with or without skews; these are called 'gabled' roofs.

I have also touched on piended roofs that have hipped slopes that meet the front and back slopes at piended joints. The photograph (see previous page) illustrates the two types of roof. The 1½ storey house on the left (pictured before) has a gabled roof (recognizable by its inverted 'V'-shaped profile) and the house on the right has a part piended roof with a hip meeting the front and back slopes at the ridge. Note that the house on the left has half round rhones passing in front of the dormer windows like the Leet Street house shown earlier on.

Another type of roof seen in Coldstream is the 'Mansard' roof, distinguishable by having a flat section at the top of the roof  joining the front and back slopes. Mansard roofs appear on Victorian houses and are sometimes difficult to see from ground level because the flat surface is hidden by the front and back slopes. The flat roofed section in the photograph (see above) is hidden to some extent by the chimneystack but the shape, extended by skews, can be seen by the profile of the gable end. There are two kinds of Mansard roof, the first having the flat section as described above and the other (which is more common on the continent of Europe) having two differently pitched roof slopes (and no flat section) known as a 'gambrel' roof.

The front elevation of the building above, at the west end of the High Street, showing the steep slope of the Mansard roof below the lead or zinc covered flat area, can be seen in the following photograph.

19th century houses with Mansard roof, High Street

The main advantage of the Mansard roof is that the flat section and steep lower slopes create more space in the attic. The houses (see above) have zinc rolls and flashings at the top of the roof slope where it joins the zinc-covered flat section and they have stone skews at both gable ends. Three separate, cast-iron 'ogee' rhones (that have a double 'S' shape in section) discharge rainwater into three cast iron, moulded hopper heads. The houses also have traditional doors and sash windows, which will be dealt with in the next chapter.

ROOFS

Traditional roofing also includes corrugated iron, which should not just be dismissed as a sub-standard, cheap and easy alternative to other forms of roofing. Corrugated iron was a British invention of the 1820s and a process of protecting the wrought iron with a zinc coating (galvanizing) was developed in the 1830s so that, by the 1840s, several manufacturers were producing it for roofing and even wall cladding. Because it was rigid and lightweight, it could be fixed directly on to unsupported timber roof frames. Corrugated iron was useful for covering large areas on farm buildings but it could also be placed on top of domestic thatch, so avoiding re-thatching whilst retaining its insulation properties. Waterproofing was obtained by overlapping sheets by two or three corrugations, laterally, and by six inches or so, vertically. Painting was essential for long-term durability. Wrought iron gave way to galvanized mild steel by the end of the century, although it was still referred to as corrugated iron.

Not a great deal of corrugated iron remains in Coldstream

 although it is still widespread on rural buildings and on industrial buildings. The example shown here (see left) is a painted, corrugated iron roof of a former barn and hayloft in Duns Road. Corrugated iron is regarded as a quality roofing material in the U.S.A., Australia and New Zealand, where shiny, galvanized sheets are in common use as an attractive architectural feature for the roofing of houses.

There are so many things to see at roof level that it is worth craning the neck, even if this results in strange glances from passers-by. Here are two to catch the eye:

Bellcote (without bell) at the old North Public School, Home Place

Bellcote (with bell and pigeon), St. Mary and All Souls Church

4

Doors and Windows

Just as the character of a human face is determined by its features, so is the facial character of an old building dependent upon the style and positioning of its doors and windows. Alter one or the other and the character will be destroyed, as has happened so often when period doors and windows have been replaced by modern 'equivalents' during the course of repair or alteration. The dressed

stone and polished ashlar frontage of the early nineteenth century former bank in the High Street (see left) is given life by the large multi-paned Georgian windows and the four-panelled door, fanlight and pilastered and corniced surround. If the windows and door were to be replaced by undivided

modern units, the effect would be to give the building's face a blank 'stare' or even worse.

Coldstream is fortunate in having retained many period doors and windows in its old buildings and this is helped by the inclusion of the old part of town in a designated Conservation Area. Section 61 of the Planning (Listed buildings and Conservation Areas) (Scotland) Act 1997 defines them as 'areas of special architectural or historic interest, the character or appearance of which it is desirable to preserve or enhance'. Buildings within a Conservation Area are subject to particular permissions and consents as to how they may be enlarged, altered, demolished or repaired and, as a result, Coldstream has retained a substantial building heritage.

Because of this, there are some interesting doors and windows to be seen in the town. The photograph shows a Victorian four-panelled door in the High Street with the door surround flanked by pilasters (see left). There is a simple over-door light. The door construction comprises the four panels with two vertical 'stiles' (or 'styles') forming the outside and inside frames of the door. There are three horizontal 'rails', the top, middle and bottom rails which connect with the stiles and there are vertical 'muntins' in the middle of the door which connect the top rail to the middle rail and the middle rail to the bottom rail.

DOORS AND WINDOWS

The design, shape and number of panels in a door can vary considerably and it is not possible to say whether any one type is traditional to Coldstream or the eastern Borders. The following illustrations show the range of design and number of panels that can be seen in the many front doors in the town. They are solidly built and their design reflects the need for security but also the fact that they are the welcoming point for visitors. They may also reflect the status of the house and the occupier. The last is a large, six-panelled, twin-leaf

door which is the north door of the Parish Church. All these doors, and there are many others, are of the period of the buildings to which they belong and any future replacement would have to be in keeping. Even where an old building is not protected by a listing or by being within a Conservation Area, the same principle applies; terrible mistakes can be made by opting for cheap, unsympathetic or out of period substitutes.

There are some excellent examples of original fanlights above front doors in the town and their survival in such good condition is a credit to the owners and occupiers of the properties. They are decorative as well as functional and some are literally fan-shaped whilst others are rectangular, over-door lights. True fanlights originated in the eighteenth century from about 1720 onwards and the most elaborate lights, with thin glazing bars or tracery, are associated particularly with Georgian architecture, although there are many Victorian designs after 1837. The earliest glazing bars were of wood, but lead or wrought iron was used later on in order to create delicate or curved patterns. In addition to those visible in the photographs on the previous page, I cannot resist including two more. Door and fanlight surrounds can be quite elaborate, but the second fanlight and

door are successfully enhanced by only a simple cornice supported by two brackets known as 'consoles'. All the doors, over-door windows and fanlights shown here are in Coldstream High Street.

Although many front doors such as the ones shown above, are imposing, as befits a main entrance, it has to be remembered that very

many workers' or simple cottages, particularly in surrounding rural areas, would have had single or double, ledged and braced doors such as the double leaf one shown here at the old Homestead at The Hirsel (see left). The doors consisted of vertical tongued and grooved boarding on the outside with top, middle and cross battens

nailed across them on the inside face of the door. On this inside face, two diagonal 'braces' would be fixed between the cross battens to provide more stability to the door, as this one in a garden at The Hirsel (see right). Ledged and braced doors would also have been used in town for some back doors, doors to outhouses and for doors in boundary walls.

In Coldstream, opening windows of the Georgian and Victorian periods were mostly, if not entirely, double-hung sash windows, i.e. the opening parts of the window (the sashes) slid up and down by means of cords and weights, rather than swinging outwards as happens with a casement window. One of the most common type

of window is the 4-pane window where the upper and lower sashes are each divided into two panes and the panes are in similar proportion to the overall window. A typical 4-pane window which can be seen almost anywhere in the town (see above) has narrow strips of wood dividing the panes called 'astragals' ('muntins' in England) and each sash frame has vertical 'stiles' and horizontal 'transoms'.

The astragals in Georgian windows are usually thinner than in Victorian windows, giving a more delicate effect. Sometimes the astragals are left out, leaving two panes only. This is common in later Victorian houses or villas with large plate glass windows. There is a rather attractive example of this in the timber-framed composite window in the High Street (see right) where the three 2-pane windows are separated by two vertical 'mullions'. This house, with the one next door is probably early nineteenth century and the window must have been a late Victorian replacement or addition.

Window sashes are not always of equal size and, in this example of a 9-pane window at Lees Cottages (see below, left), the

upper sash of six panes slides over a lower sash of three panes. Other than the 4-pane window, perhaps the most traditional window in Coldstream, Berwickshire, the Lothians and up into Fife and beyond, is the 12-pane window (see next page) which has two equally sized sashes of six panes each. The thin astragals and transoms suggest that this one could be an original Georgian window dating from the

55

early part of the nineteenth century. Compare the delicacy of the astragals with the more substantial ones in the 9-pane cottage window above.

However, it is not possible to be hard and fast about what is the most traditional design of window in this area. Here is an

example of a two-sash, 16-pane window in the High Street (see left). The uneven rybats give it a cottage feel, in keeping with the random rubble walling. The sill and lintel have been replaced at some time.

Windows come in all shapes and sizes in Coldstream. There is an attractive window with three, arched panes on the High Street near the Leet Water bridge (see right). This window is underneath the composite window mentioned earlier and is set in a very shallow (Victorian or later), timber bay window, in a much earlier nineteenth

century house. Just around the corner, facing the Leet Water is a stylish end bow with composite windows on both storeys (see below). A set of three windows such as each of these, with a central arched window which is taller and usually wider than the two flanking windows, is known as a 'Venetian window' or a 'Palladian window' because it is based upon the designs of the seventeenth century Venetian architect, Andrea Palladio. Many Georgian churches had this form of window in their east end. The central windows also have two prominent, projecting and decorative 'key stones' at the top of the arched windows.

Composite 'Venetian' windows at the Leet Water Bridge

I mentioned bay windows before. These were first introduced in the sixteenth century, but they enjoyed a surge in popularity during the late Victorian and Edwardian eras.

Detached late Victorian house on the corner of Tweed Terrace

The house above has quite shallow, square bay windows on the left and polygonal bays on the right. Apart from being an architectural feature, a bay window increased the floor area of a room and, particularly in the case of a polygonal bay, increased the amount of light flooding in from outside. The windows above are typical, large, Victorian 2-pane sash windows and have carved, chamfered and moulded surrounds. Straying from the windows for a moment, it is worth noting the door surround with its prominent panelled stone pilasters, panelled arch and corbelled plinth across the top. There is a Mansard roof and piended roofs above the bay windows. This type of Mansard roof has slopes on all sides up to the flat section, whereas the house discussed in Chapter 3 had gabled ends on either side with slopes only at front and back. Other features to be seen are the stone brackets below the slated roof with its zinc flashings and the ashlar frontage with projecting inband and outband quoins.

Getting back to windows again, moulded details were often applied above doors and windows and these can have a practical as well as a decorative purpose. For example, drip mouldings above and to the side of the lintel, date back to at least the fifteenth century in domestic architecture and into medieval times in church architecture. They divert rainwater running down the face of the wall to prevent drips and also provide an attractive architectural feature that complements the door or window. This one (see above) is on the old North Public School on the south side of Home Place and dates from 1900, but matches one on the adjoining building, which dates from 1858.

The Marjoribanks family, their architect and builders certainly created an unusual late eighteenth century building for the Lees estate at 'The Dovecote', between Duke Street and Leet Street.

The photograph (see left) shows part of the building with its gothic windows and doors on the ground floor and an attractive quatrefoil window in the battlemented tower.

Perhaps the building was designed with an ecclesiastical feel to it to reflect the fact that it was on part of, or near to the site of, Coldstream Priory, but I have no evidence to support this.

Attics without dormer windows received minimal light and

air from roof lights and, from the mid nineteenth century onwards, these were often 2-pane cast iron framed roof lights. Many survive and this one (see left) is hinged along the top and should still have its metal 'stay' at the bottom allowing it to be propped open for ventilation.

It is interesting to see the amount of old glass that survives in Coldstream windows, recognized by its distortion and wavy lines. This might be 'crown glass' or 'cylinder glass'. Crown glass, which was common in the eighteenth century, although still made through into the twentieth century, was made by mouth-blowing a sphere which was then opened out at one end and spun into a flat disc. Several panes of crown glass could be cut out of each disc with the best glass coming from the outer portion of the disc. Crown windows were often slightly bowed as a result of a secondary cooling process.

Cylinder glass, which was commonly used in the nineteenth century, was mouth-blown into a bottle-shaped cylinder from which the two ends were cut off. The cylinder was then reheated and unrolled to give a flat piece of glass, which was allowed to cool slowly.

Also during the nineteenth century, large areas of 'polished plate glass' for grander windows were made from slab glass, polished on both sides. It was a very flat type of glass but it was an expensive process. In the twentieth century, 'drawn sheet glass' was produced by lifting molten glass in sheet form out of a vat and passing it through rollers. Modern glass windows are made of 'float glass', which is made by floating molten glass over a bed of tin. It is very accurate in its dimensions and it can be produced in long lengths.

Domestic windows are not the only ones to be seen in the town. There are some interesting examples of workshop windows, such as these in an old building to the west of the old Coldstream Brewery site (see above). There is another such example in Duke Street. Fixed light (i.e. non-opening) windows such as these were commonly used for workshops, mills and smiddies in Scotland in the eighteenth and nineteenth centuries. The frames and astragals could be of wood or of metal (cast iron or zinc) and the large windows were designed to admit plenty of light rather than air. The long, vertical astragals hold overlapping panes of glass without horizontal fixing and the small size of the panes may reflect the method of producing comparatively small flat glass sheets from cylinder glass. Alternatively, the practical reason may be that if something or someone broke the window in a working environment, it was cheaper and easier to replace small overlapping panes rather than the whole window. Very often, I have a tendency to speculate!

Coldstream retains many Victorian and Edwardian shop window fronts. Some have been modified in the distant past, such as

the addition of granite pillars at W. E. Howden's pet food suppliers shop, at the beginning of the twentieth century (see left). In some cases, sub-divided shop windows dating from Georgian times would have been replaced by polished plate glass windows from the mid

1800s and by float glass windows in more recent times. However, these and other modifications have not been allowed to detract from the original design and, for example at Howden's, the granite pillars have added to the character.

Shop front surrounds comprising the entablature, columns, plinths, capitals and corbelled brackets were in stone and timber and it is quite surprising how well the timber elements have survived including detailed carving such as the pilaster capitals at the pharmacy (see previous page).

Four of Coldstream's unspoilt shopfronts in the High Street

Shopfronts were not confined to the High Street because, although Market Square (Place) gradually lost its prominence as Coldstream's 'hub' after the construction of Coldstream Bridge and the development of the High Street, many shops, businesses and public houses remained there right through into the twentieth century. Only three shops (and no pubs) survive in the Square and in Market Street; they all retain their character from the nineteenth century. The

shopfront of the gift shop in Market Street (see above, left) is almost the same as it was when Brydon's butcher's shop was there in the nineteenth century. The Berwickshire Association for Voluntary Service in Market Square (Place) also retains its nineteenth century

shopfront with the original fascia covered and protected by the Association's sign. A detail of the timber shopfront surround (see above, right) shows one of the classical capitals with its decorative corbels, to the left of the fascia. Recently, the former sweetshop then fishing tackle shop in Market Square has become a jewellery workshop (see above). The shop window is post World War II.

A number of former shops have been subsumed or converted into housing. The eighteenth century house at 'Toun Heid' (see next page) had William Henderson's drapery shop added in the nineteenth century; the shop was later closed and taken back into the house with two Victorian sash windows being added to the infilled shopfront.

The former shop in the High Street, now a private house (see

below), was once occupied by George W. Gibson's photography shop. The timber shopfront bay windows have not altered since that time but the shop door has been infilled and the stonework frontage and door surround to the right have been painted over. The large windows below the smaller panes were there at the beginning of the twentieth century, but the design with its two bay windows on either side of the shop door (now a window) is reminiscent of shopfronts of a much earlier period in the nineteenth century and I

wonder whether the lower windows were originally sub-divided. Another house to the left of this one (not shown) also had a shop in the nineteenth century and through into the twentieth century.

65

Early photographs also show that, in the early years of the twentieth century, William Haig's biscuit and bread-making shop was in one of the former Coldstream Brewery managers' houses in Market Place. The shop has now gone, but its position can still be seen in the photograph (see above) where the infill stonework in the centre of the ground floor can only just be made out, such was the quality of the masonry infill. This quality is confirmed in the replacement window, which has been installed with matching carved lintel. Note the different style of the first floor lintels, the 4-pane sash windows and the contrast between the ashlar facing with its 'string course' and the different surface treatment of the dressed, coursed stonework on the next-door house. The gabled, slated roof has skews and there is a brick chimneystack with an oversailing course and two circular cans.

There are quite a number of old buildings in Coldstream that have blocked up windows. This may be a legacy of successive window taxes that were first levied in England during the seventeenth century and in Scotland in the eighteenth century. The tax was levied on a scale determined by the number of windows in the house and this was eventually fixed at above seven windows, payable by the occupiers of the property. Occupiers often used to blank off windows

in various ways in order to reduce or avoid paying tax. In Scotland, some occupiers used to paint white astragals on to a black painted background (see left) and, particularly in Edinburgh, these were often known disparagingly as 'Pitt's Pictures' after the Prime Minister, William Pitt the Younger, who increased the tax in 1784, 1797 and 1802. In 1850, Viscount Duncan, when presenting petitions in the House of Commons for the repeal of window tax, gave as examples the tax on an 8-windowed house at 18s. 1d. and the tax on a 39-windowed mansion at £14 16s. 2d. (Hansard HC Apr. 1850, vol. 110 cc. 68-99). The vote went against him by three votes, but the tax was abolished anyway, the following year.

Some of the blanked out or infilled windows, in addition to the one above, are shown below, but—a note of caution, because it is not possible to say with certainty whether these particular windows in Coldstream were blocked off because of the window tax, but my feeling is that this was the reason.

5

Bits and Pieces

The unique character of Coldstream's 'old town' has been determined by the varied designs, irregular layout and different uses of its buildings over the centuries, all of which reflect the historical development of the community. Previous chapters have dealt with the *visible structural and essential elements* of buildings and the traditional materials that were used in their makeup and have highlighted the richly varied frontages and roofscapes that have made the town what it is.

This chapter deals with some of the 'extras' which add to the appearance of buildings, but which are often taken for granted or overlooked. Not many people stop to examine them, as familiarity means that they only form part of the overall picture, but they are always worth looking at more closely, if time permits. In addition to these, I will also mention some 'add-on' or 'stand alone' items, because they are interesting in themselves and come within a loose description of 'buildings', if buildings are considered to be all things constructed and not just structures enclosed by walls and a roof.

Buildings are always enhanced by the appropriate use of cast and wrought iron for railings, gates, lamp brackets, finials and other ornamental decoration. Many eighteenth and nineteenth century examples survive in Coldstream despite the large-scale removal of railings for recycling into munitions during the Second World War, as a result of a national appeal by the Minister of Aircraft Production, Lord Beaverbrook. Whether or not the railings were ever used for this purpose has led to ongoing discussion, but there is little doubt that their removal was a morale boosting exercise for the population. Railings that were needed to protect hazardous areas were not removed and, in the High Street, there are surviving railings, surrounding basement wells and flanking flyover and other steps.

High Street, north side, has a variety of original iron railings

Cast iron and wrought iron differ from each other in their composition and method of manufacture. Cast iron is smelted quickly at high temperatures and contains more impurities than wrought iron and, in particular, it has a higher carbon content than wrought iron. Because of this, it is more prone to rusting and is also hard and brittle, so it will break quite easily if struck by, say, a hammer. Wrought iron is a purer form of iron and is smelted more slowly at a lower temperature in order to remove the impurities, meaning that it is softer and can be literally 'wrought' or worked into shape using tools. It is less hard than cast iron but it is still tough, yet malleable, and is therefore useful for bending into intricate shapes. It can also be welded, which is not possible with cast iron.

Original iron railings, west end of High Street

Original iron railings, central High Street

Wrought iron may be considered a more suitable material for outdoor work because of its better resistance to rust, its malleability and its resistance to knocks, but railings, gates and other structures were (and still are) also made of cast iron. Cast iron is the product of a metalworking process, whereas wrought iron is the result of the blacksmith's art, but both forms need the skill of the designer and the skill of the forger or caster. It is often difficult to tell wrought iron and cast iron apart, but one clue to look for is the welding used to join pieces of wrought iron. Also, cast iron can be identified where two moulded casts have been joined together, leaving a tell-tale seam down both sides. This is easily seen, for example, down the side of

cast iron rhone pipes but it is not so easy to see on railings and gates when the ironwork has been repeatedly painted over the years. However, it doesn't really matter whether it is wrought iron or cast iron, if the end result is good.

Coldstream retains a good variety of railings and other ironwork and the photographs show some that

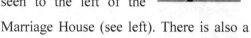

are worth looking out for. There are some large gates in and around the town and I have included a detail of the scrollwork on top of the gates to be seen to the left of the Marriage House (see left). There is also a

lighting bracket

on the wall of the Newcastle Arms (see right) that perhaps lit a recent Inn sign. In the early twentieth century, there used to be an Inn sign close to this and, in the 1920s there was an Automobile Association sign in roughly that position.

The Coldstream War Memorial was unveiled in 1923 and the iron gates and railings that were made locally, complement the solidity and strength of the sandstone monument. There are no flowing lines here and the ironwork is formed from rectangular rods that have been used to great effect (see left and below). The railings incorporate a lion's head and they also echo the classical 'key' pattern (seen to the left of the lion's head) around the central monolith.

Coldstream War Memorial, unveiled 1923

Ironwork is often to be found on the roofs of buildings in the form of finials on top of dormer window roofs or, as in this example (see below), as a weathervane. This one includes a great deal of wrought ironwork in various forms including rods, scrollwork and hammered coronet, vane and compass cardinal points. It would probably have been made by the blacksmith on The Hirsel estate and includes the 'H' for the Earls of Home.

Weathervane on top of the dovecote, The Hirsel Visitor Centre

Iron railings are not only found at ground floor level—this example (see below) of a decorative iron railing as part of a balustrade can be seen over the porch at Victoria Lodge in the High Street. Balustrades are more commonly built of stone, like the renaissance style balustrade over the door to Halifax Bank of Scotland

and so this stone and iron one is an unusual and effective addition to the Lodge porch. The regularity and style of the ironwork suggests to me that it is made of cast iron rather than wrought iron.

I just had to include a photograph (see left) of the cast iron Victorian post box, set into the wall of the present Police Station at the junction of High Street and Lennel Road. I think it may be of a style made between 1881 and 1904 because front collection tablets were not introduced until 1881. It is not, of course unique to Coldstream, but I mention it because it is still in daily use.

There are quite a number of inscriptions attached to or incised into buildings or onto structures in the town and it is interesting to note the variety of purposes for which they exist. The War Memorial heads the list because of its purpose and its significance to the town; thereafter, the following plaques and inscriptions may be seen roughly in sequence, travelling from south-west to north-east. I have included some which are modern or relatively modern, in order to try to provide a comprehensive list, but there may well be others:-

1. Coldstream War Memorial to those who gave their lives in the Great War, the Second World War and, by association, in later conflicts. Unveiled by Fld. Mar. Douglas Haig, 1st Earl Haig, 1923.

2. Coldstream Medical Centre. A commemorative, slate fountain 'in honour of the founders, local community, patients and staff, Coldstream Cottage Hospital 1888-2008'.

3. Monument on The Hirsel estate to the 11th Earl of Home who collapsed and died in the woods in 1881.

4. Obelisk on The Hirsel estate, erected in 1784 with inscriptions in memory of William, Lord Dunglass, son of the 9th Earl of Home, who died of wounds received at the battle of Guilford Court House during the American War of Independence.

5. Statue and commemorative stones at the entrance to The Hirsel, in honour of Sir Alec Douglas-Home, 14th Earl of Home.

4. Coldstream West United Free Church (Community Centre), High Street: foundation stone laid by Mrs. Black, Lanton, July 5th 1906.

5. Coldstream Parish Church, High Street: foundation stone laid by the Rt. Hon. The Lady Clementine Waring of Lennel, 27th September 1906.

6. Granite obelisk in front of Coldstream Parish Church in honour of Sir John Marjoribanks of Lees who gifted 'an abundant and permanent supply of water' in 1852.

7. Plaque, Tweed Road, marking the headquarters of the Coldstream Guards, 1659, rebuilt 1865.

8. Plaque, Adam Thomson Court, off Tweed Road (see above).

9. Two plaques on the former North Public School in Home Place giving the completion dates of two building phases in 1858 and 1900.

10. Plaque, Nursery Lane, commemorating the opening of 12 flats at Hirsel Court by Lord Home of the Hirsel, 21st April 1989.

11. Coldstream Free Church (Eildon Centre), Victoria Street: plaque commemorating the foundation in 1846, the extension and renovation in 1891 and the gift of tower, clock and bell by Thomas Hogg, J.P. of Hope Park.

12. Plaque, Henderson Park, commemorating the visit of HM The Queen and HRH The Duke of Edinburgh on 5th July 1962. Unveiled by Sir Alex (sic) Douglas-Home, KT., PC., MP., Prime Minister. 5th August 1964.

Stone presented to the Burgh by the Coldstream Guards, 1968

13. Stone, Henderson Park, presented to the Burgh by the Coldstream Guards, 1968 (see previous page). The base holds pebbles inscribed in memory of Guardsmen killed in Afghanistan.

14. Two slate monuments above Tweed Green, erected by the Flodden 1513 Club, describing the journey of the Scottish army to Flodden, the result of the battle in 1513 and the return of many noblemen at the cause of Isabella Hoppringle, Abbess, (of Coldsteam Priory) to be buried in consecrated ground.

15. Stone monument above Tweed Green, topped by a stone sword pointing to Flodden Field, erected by the Flodden 1513 Club and inscribed, 'The Flowers of the Forest that fought aye the foremost The prime o' our land are cauld in the clay'.

Commemorative and memorial sword pointing over the River Tweed to the site of the Battle of Flodden, 1513

16. Plaque inset into boundary wall above Tweed Green, marking the flood levels of the River Tweed on 9th February 1831 and 3rd August 1948.

17. Plaque at base of monument, Tweed Terrace, erected by friends of Charles Marjoribanks, Esq. MP., in admiration of his talents and to commemorate the victory of the Independent Liberal Electors of Berwickshire, 1832.

18. Plaque set into Marriage House, Coldstream Bridge 'Weddings conducted here until 1856 Restored 1957'.

19. Plaque, north-east parapet, Coldstream Bridge, informing that the bridge was built at a cost of £6,000 between 1763 and 1766. Foundations were protected with concrete, parapet walls rebuilt and the cauld (the weir) repaired 1922. The bridge was strengthened by reinforced concrete arches and widened by cantilevering the footpaths 1960-61. Gives names of trustees and engineers.

The Robert Burns Commemorative Plaque (see next page)

20. Plaque, south-west parapet, Coldstream Bridge, erected by Coldstream Burns Club, May 7th 1926 to commemorate Robert Burns' crossing into England for the first time, 7th May 1787 (see previous page).

> 'O SCOTIA! MY DEAR, MY NATIVE SOIL!
> FOR WHOM MY WARMEST WISH TO HEAVEN IS SENT!
> LONG MAY THY HARDY SONS OF RUSTIC TOIL
> BE BLEST WITH HEALTH, AND PEACE, AND SWEET CONTENT.'

21. Church of St. Mary and All Souls, Lennel Road: foundation stone laid by the Right Rev. George, Bishop of Edinburgh, Feasts of S. S. Simon and Jude, 1913.

Coldstream buildings have some small period features that are worth looking out for and which can often be overlooked. The photograph (see below) shows one of them. From the early twentieth century onwards, the streets of Coldstream were surfaced with tarmacadam and later, with bitumen. Before that, the streets were

sometimes cobbled, such as in Market Place, or covered in stone, gravel and sand; at worst, they were just hard-packed clay or mud. Horses deposited large amounts of dung that was churned up and mixed into the street surface by passing carts, forming a glutinous combination, made even worse in wet weather. The construction of pavements helped the pedestrian to some extent, but streets had to be crossed, and the wearing of boots and the lifting of skirts were necessary precautions against the mess. Entry to houses would have been impossible without having cast iron boot scrapers at the front door, many of them ornamental and bolted to the step. However, the majority were considered to be so essential that they were often purely utilitarian in design and built in to the fabric of the house like the one shown, which is to the side of a doorway next to the newsagents' shop in the High Street. It still has its horizontal bar intact, as many others have been rusted away over the years.

Other survivals to look for are old coal chute hatches, such as this one set in to the wall of Victoria Lodge in Nursery Lane. Coal would have been delivered to basement coal cellars either through a pavement or forecourt chute having a cast iron cover or, very often, through a chute with an opening in the side of the  building having a hinged wooden hatch door. There are many examples still to be seen in Coldstream; some have been infilled with brick and stone but often the outline of the opening can be traced in the stonework.

Iron and brass door and entrance furniture has often been replaced over time but there are many original items in the town that are still in use. I have included a selection of door knockers, handles, a letter box and a bell-pull. Some of them are obviously original, others are at least old and some may just be good reproductions, but they are all decorative and practical, are in keeping with their location, and I like them for their own sake. They are not the only

83

ones to be seen. The cast iron bell-pull near the pharmacy in the High Street is probably a survival from the days before electric bell-pushes.

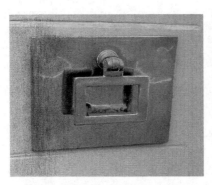

The door handle (see below, left) has matching escutcheon plates for covering the key-holes.

Antique door furniture is not restricted to domestic buildings and these old brass door guard/handles, letterbox and grab handle (see below) have survived over the years and can be seen on or near the shop door of R. Carmichael & Sons in the High Street.

Boundary walls often incorporate stone gateposts; three are

shown here that are all one of a pair; the first (see left) is at the entrance to the estate offices at The Hirsel and is representative of many solid gateposts to be found in the area, with tooled projecting masonry blocks with a capping stone. It is functional yet decorative and fulfils its intended purpose of marking the entrance to buildings which were important to the running of the estate.

The second is at the lower entrance to Lennel House, below Belmont House and near the Marriage House (see right). The post is similar but it has a dentilated classical capping

topped by a ball finial, reflecting a much grander entrance on to the road between Coldstream Bridge and the town.

The third (see left) is at the entrance to The Lees and has an ashlar column with an oversailing course and a plain capping stone, although a projecting nib suggests that, at one time, there may have been a ball or other finial on top. There are attractive floriated panels, front and back, set on to a frieze with mouldings, above and below. This is an early gatepost, which probably dates back to the building of the eighteenth century house.

In contrast to the imposing entrance gateposts to be found in the town, here is a very old field post near Swinton that is an example of a style to be found throughout the Borders (see right). It may not herald the entrance to a grand house but it is still impressive and is one of a number of such posts along the stretch of road between the village and the quarry. This post and other similar ones would have reflected the status of the estate owners who wished to mark the entrances  and boundaries of their fields with such attractive, shaped, circular stonework pillars and 'mushroom' caps. Their survival to the present day is due to their solidity, functionality and pleasing appearance.

I have not made any great distinction between urban and rural building features because Coldstream and nearby villages and settlements have always been part of the rural scene. In the past, employment in Coldstream depended to a large degree on agriculture and associated trades and industries. Times have changed, but connections are still strong and I consider Coldstream to be part of the countryside, with many rural features in and around the town.

As part of the change, old farm buildings that were once used for storage of carts and machinery have often been converted for modern uses. Cart stores had wide 'segmental' arches such as the

arches at the pottery at The Hirsel Visitor Centre (see left). The spaces have been infilled with random rubble below the recent windows. The entrances to stable and carriage buildings were

much higher with more rounded arches, such as the main entrance and infilled arches at the former Lees stables which have been converted to housing (see right). The attractive eighteenth century central portion has a battlemented upper storey with blind quatrefoil decoration. Note the four string courses and the piended roofs on either side of the central portion.

Dovecotes (doocots) were built to house pigeons or doves with large ones, such as that at what is now the Hirsel Visitor Centre, being used by estates for keeping birds for their meat, eggs and droppings. They might have beehive or vaulted roofs, or the roof might have a single south-facing slope, with the doocot then being called a 'lectern doocot'. The small doocot built into the roof of a

house in Birgham (see left) is very typical of many domestic ones that can still be seen in rural areas in the Borders. Also on the theme of birds, it was always good practice to build owl holes into the gable ends of barns or attic roofs

of rural buildings in order that the resident owls could keep down vermin. The one shown here (see right) can be seen from the main street in Birgham.

There are so many 'bits and pieces' to see in Coldstream and

I have only touched on some of them. There will be others that are familiar to people who see them every day, but there is scope for everyone to discover something new, however familiar they may be with the town's nooks and crannies. That is why, for me, it is so interesting to walk down the passages and steps and along the riverside walks, keeping a good lookout. An example is the dark, narrow, upper end of the 'dog-legged' Gas Lane (see above). After it leaves the cottages at the High Street end, it becomes more open beyond, as it passes by Gowanlea. At the second

'dog-leg' there is an old iron bracket set in the angle, which looks as though it may have held a gas lamp or an early electric street lamp (see right).

Descent of the narrow passage leading down to Bluebell Steps or the even narrower passage between high walls leading from Leet Street to Penitents Walk reveals random rubble walling which

oozes age. A real sense of history arises when walking along Nun's Walk and Penitents Walk, looking at the boundary walls. Another advantage of exploring these passages and walks is that it is possible to see buildings and outbuildings from different or unusual angles.

Bluebell Steps leading to Nun's Walk and Tweed Green

The walls alongside Nun's Walk and up to Braeheads have suffered a great deal from landslips over the years and have been rebuilt and patched up so many times that much of the stonework has been altered or obscured by cement repairs. The history is still there underneath, but the stones alongside Penitents Walk can be seen more easily and there are sections that still retain old lime mortar bedding joints. Countless alterations have been made and old openings filled in, but the ancient walls allow for free rein of the imagination.

The Penitents Walk wall is roughly built to courses (see next page) but, in addition to random rubble, many of the stones are very regular in shape and some, despite weathering over time, still retain signs of stugging or other decorative finish. In the photographs (see page 92), the coping stones and the stones below them show this very

The narrow passage and steps leading down to Penitents Walk

The wall alongside Penitents Walk

Detail of the wall alongside Penitents Walk

well and there are others like them elsewhere in the wall. This leads me to wonder whether they are reused stones, albeit from a very long time ago, and that they might have come from Coldstream Priory in the early seventeenth century, after its closure and abandonment. More speculation!

Finally, I always think that a good starting point in appreciating a town is to look at the stonework, as other things will flow from that—and not just the obvious dressed stonework, but the rubble walls, the garden and boundary walls, the copings and the gateposts, all with their mixed styles and shapes. I have been accused of being somewhat obsessive about stones and walls and I suppose that is true. It must be the reason why I started the first chapter writing about them and why I am still writing about them at the end of this last chapter, with many references in between.

GLOSSARY

apse—semicircular or polygonal end wall of a chancel.

arris—the external corner formed by the meeting of two walls

ashlar—stones cut into rectangular blocks, polished or finely tooled, with fine mortar beds.

astragal—a bar which divides a window sash into smaller panes.

bedding plane—the natural horizontal layers of sedimentary rock laid down by water many millions of years ago. Also, a bed is the horizontal mortar joint in stonework.

bevel—a vertical or horizontal sloping surface, edge or angle in masonry or carpentry.

broaching—the tooling of the face of dressed stone with a chisel or boaster to give a finish of parallel lines.

can—Scottish term for a chimneypot of fired clay or metal.

capital—the head feature of a classical column.

casement—a side-hinged window.

cement mortar—a modern bonding and pointing material for stonework and brickwork using cement and sand.

chamfer—a surface formed by cutting off a sharp edge or corner.

collar—a horizontal timber connecting the truss beams which support the roof rafters.

common brick—a brick made for general building purposes.

console—an ornamental scrolled supporting bracket in stone or timber.

coping—the top course of masonry on a wall

corbel—a bracket supporting a cornice.

corbie-step—stone stepped ends on top of a gable wall, rather than a sloping skew.

cornice—a flat-topped ledge with moulding or brackets below.

GLOSSARY

course—a row of stones in a wall, of similar height.

courser—squared or rectangular stone laid with others in courses in a wall.

cowl—a hood-shaped (usually) cover for a chimney or ventilator.

daub—clay applied to a timber-framed wattle wall.

dentil—a small square block used in series in classical cornices.

doric—the simplest form of the classical orders.

dormer—a window wholly or partly set in a sloping roof, having its own roof and
    side walls.

dressed stonework—regular masonry tooled to a finished state.

drip—a projection moulding that prevents rainwater running down the face of a wall.

droving—see **broaching**.

fanlight—a semicircular or rectangular window over a door or another window.

fillet—a triangular profile flashing of cement and sand or lime and sand in the angle
    between roof and wall.

finial—an ornament in stone, timber or metal at the apex of a dormer or ridge.

flashing—a zinc or lead apron or fillet over a joint between masonry and slates or
    tiles.

flaunching—the sloping mortar fillet on top of a chimneystack in which chimney
    cans are set and which allows rainwater to run off.

frieze—the middle section of a classical entablature (cornice, frieze, architrave).

gable—the end wall of a building.

gambrel roof—a gable or piended roof with two slopes, front and back.

harling—an external wall coating of lime and sand with aggregate thrown on.

hip—a sloping end to a gable, resulting in a pyramid shape instead of a pointed
    gable.

hopper—a funnel, often ornamented, which collects rainwater from a rhone for
    discharge into a rhone pipe.

ionic—a classical order. An ionic capital has spiral scrolls (volutes).

inband—the shorter headed rybat

key pattern—a repetitive angular classical pattern

keystone—the central shaped stone in an arch or vault.

lie-in—the sloping ceilings in an attic or part attic room.

lime mortar—a traditional bonding and pointing material for stonework, using lime and sand.

lintel—a stone or timber beam over a window or door opening.

mansard—the roof is flat on top and slopes down steeply on two or four sides. In continental Europe, it has two slopes on each side, the lower being steeper than the upper—in effect, a gambrel roof.

margin—a flat or tooled border worked in stone around a door or window opening or at the corner of a building.

mullion—a vertical member between close but separate windows.

muntin—the central vertical frame on a panelled door.

oculus—a circular opening.

ogee—a moulding in stone, joinery, or cast iron with two reverse curves in section like a letter S.

outband—the longer headed rybat, compared with the inband.

oversailing course—a course of stonework or brickwork projecting in front of the face of the chimneystack.

pantile—a roof tile of S section.

pediment—a triangular classical gable or an ornamental feature resembling it.

piend—the joint between a hipped roof slope and a front or back roof slope.

pilaster—a rectangular or part circular, undetached classical column.

pinnings—small stone slithers used to fill gaps and level up a course.

plinth—a base or platform which supports a column, monument or other structure.

portico—a porch with the roof and pediment supported by columns.

purlin—timber strut spanning horizontally across rafters to carry roofing.

quatrefoil—a four-lobed opening as a window or within tracery.

quoin—a dressed stone at the angle of a building.

rail—a horizontal frame member on a panelled door.

random rubble—rough undressed stonework.

rebate—a hidden rectangular section cut out of masonry to take a door or window frame.

reveal—the visible return face of stonework at a window or door opening.

rhone—a gutter along the eaves for rainwater.

ridge—the apex of a roof.

roll—a moulding, circular in section, formed by a metal roofing joint.

GLOSSARY

roundel—a circular ornamental stonework or other feature.

rustication—an exaggerated form of masonry with recessed or V-shaped joints.

rybat—a dressed stone used in forming corners at door and window openings.

sarking—timber boarding laid over rafters, to which the roof covering is fixed.

sash—a vertically sliding window with hidden balancing weights on rope or chain.

segmental arch—an arch where the curve of the arch is less than a semi-circlular
   segment of a circle.

sill (cill)—a single stone slab beneath a window.

skew—the raking top of a gable projecting above the roof, topped by coping stones.

skewputt—the lowest stone at the foot of a skew, built into the wall below, for
   strength.

sneck—a small square stone built into masonry, with others, to level up a course.

spalling—the splitting away of the face of stonework due to frost or damp.

start—a vertical rybat at the side of a door or window used in conjunction with tails
   to provide a bond with the adjoining masonry.

stile—the vertical side member of a panelled door or a window.

string course—a decorative horizontal band of stone or brick projecting beyond or
   flush with the face of a building.

stugging—a picked, surface tooling in dressed stonework.

tail—a single rybat at the side of a door or window used in conjunction with starts to
   provide a bond with the adjoining masonry.

tracery—masonry patterns used in the framework of openings such as elaborate
   church windows.

transom—horizontal member separating window lights.

truss—framework of timber which, with others, supports the longitudal supports for
   roof rafters.

tympanum—the flat surface between a lintel and an arch or within a pediment.

verge—the board on the top of a gable where there is no skew and the roof projects
   over the wallhead.

voussoir—a wedge-shaped stone used with others to form an arch.

wattle—a timber-framed wall with flexible branches woven through and often
   covered in clay (daub).